Read & Respond

Ages
5~7

CW00461046

PAGE
1

Read & Respond

Ages 5–7

Author: Jean Evans

Commissioning Editor: Rachel Mackinnon

Development Editor: Marion Archer

Assistant Editor: Rachel Coombs

Series Designer: Anna Oliwa

Designer: Tracey Camden

Illustrations: Mike Lacey (Beehive Illustration)

Text © 2012, Jean Evans © 2012, Scholastic Ltd

Designed using Adobe InDesign

Published by Scholastic Ltd,
Book End, Range Road, Witney,
Oxfordshire OX29 0YD
www.scholastic.co.uk

Printed by Bell & Bain
1 2 3 4 5 6 7 8 9   2 3 4 5 6 7 8 9 0 1

British Library Cataloguing-in-Publication Data
A catalogue record for this book is available from
the British Library.
ISBN 978-1407-12725-5

Acknowledgements

The publishers gratefully acknowledge permission to reproduce the following copyright material: **Macmillan Children's Books** for the use of text extracts, illustrations and the cover from *The Room on the Broom* by Julia Donaldson, illustrated by Axel Scheffler. Text © 2001, Julia Donaldson; Illustrations © 2001 Axel Scheffler. (2001, Macmillan Children's Books). Every effort has been made to trace copyright holders for the works reproduced in this book, and the publishers apologise for any inadvertent omissions.

Room on the Broom

About the book

Room on the Broom tells the story of a friendly witch and her faithful cat who enjoy flying around, watching the world go by – that is until the day that the wind blows the witch's hat right off her head. Luckily a keen dog bounds from the bushes with the hat in his mouth and asks to ride on the broom and… *whoosh!*, off they fly. But it is not long before the witch loses her bow and then her wand. Again, the witch is in luck as a green bird and a clean frog retrieve them. To show how grateful she is, the witch makes room on her broom for them all. Then calamity strikes as the broom snaps, the passengers tumble downwards into a bog and a fiery dragon licks his lip at the thought of *WITCH AND CHIPS*! Bravely, the witch's new friends disguise themselves as a horrible beast to scare away the cowardly dragon and rescue the witch. The wonderful climax to the story sees *A TRULY MAGNIFICENT BROOM* rise from the witch's cauldron, cleverly accessorised with something for everyone.

This book will inspire children's imaginations to soar as they fly with the witch and her friends, share her encounter with a fearsome dragon and create their own designs for truly magnificent brooms. It will help to develop children's ability to appreciate and experiment with the effects of rich patterned language, rollicking rhyme and satisfying repetition. The book will also raise children's awareness of the importance of true friendship as they consider how the characters clearly support one another.

About the author

Julia Donaldson was born on 16 September 1948 and brought up in a musical household. Julia attended the University of Bristol and during her university years she went busking around Europe.

The busking, supported by her wonderful rhyme and language skills, led to a career in singing and songwriting, mainly for BBC children's television. Of all of Julia's characters, perhaps the most popular is *The Gruffalo,* whose inspiration has roots in Chinese folklore.

Julia was appointed as the seventh Children's Laureate in June 2011. She plans to tour libraries and extend children's involvement in drama and music, using her natural skills and ability to inhabit their imaginative worlds.

About the illustrator

Axel Scheffler has collaborated on picture books with Julia Donaldson since the publication of *A Squash and a Squeeze,* but he is also the best-selling illustrator of books such as *The Bedtime Bear* and *The Tickle Book.* His distinctive characters and humorous details bounce from every page and perfectly enhance Julia Donaldson's unique and wonderful verse. Probably the character he is most known for in his partnership with Julia is *The Gruffalo,* and other popular characters include *Tiddler, Stick Man* and *Tabby McTat.*

Facts and figures
Published in 2001.
Adapted into a children's puppet show at the Edinburgh Festival in 2009, the show then moved to the West End in January 2010 and is now touring the UK.

Guided reading

Introducing the book

Show the children the front cover of the book before starting to read, so that they can focus on the illustration in order to make predictions about the story. Begin by reading the title and ask: *Can you tell from the title what the story might be about? Who would be likely to need room on a broom? What do you notice about the words* room *and* broom*? What might this tell us about the way the story is told?* (It might be in rhyme.)

Draw attention to the names Julia Donaldson and Axel Scheffler and ask if the children have heard of either of them. Establish who is the author and who is the illustrator of the book. (To extend this discussion, find out more on page 3.) Encourage the children to name some other titles that they have read by Julia Donaldson and discuss what they know about her style. (For example, that the stories are often funny and usually in rhyme.) Look at the illustration on the cover, especially the facial expressions of the characters, and ask if this distinctive style reminds them of the work of Axel Scheffler in any other books.

Closely explore the illustrations on the front and back cover together. Focus on the image of the witch and the background landscape and ask the children: *Who do you think is the main character in the story? Where do you think she might be going on her broom? Who is travelling with her? What time of day is it?* Then turn to the image of the dragon on the back cover. Ask: *What part might this character play in the story? Does the owl's expression help us to decide whether this is a fierce or friendly dragon?*

Next, read the text on the back cover, which is taken from the first page of the story. Ask: *What do these words say about the main character? Do they make you want to find out where the witch and her cat are going? Which two words give clues about the mood of the witch and the cat?* (They should pick out *purred* and *grinned*.) *What evidence is there that the story might be in rhyme?* Read the quote from *The Independent* and discuss the meaning of the words *another gem*. Ask: *What is a gem? Why might this book be described as a* gem?

Initial reading

Ensure that your initial reading of *Room on the Broom* captures the imaginations of the children as they share in a lively and engaging experience and develop their initial impressions. Read clearly and expressively, encouraging participation. (For example, pausing so that they can join in with predictable rhyming words or asking them to shout the angry words of the dragon and beast together.) Vary vocal tone and body language to build up mood and atmosphere. (For instance, saying the word *whoosh!* while moving an arm up in the air to indicate the speed and direction of the disappearing broom.)

Use body movements to engage children in the actions of the characters, such as holding a hand to shield your eyes to indicate searching or imitating a tight 'clutching' motion by making a fist to show anger. Introduce varied and consistent voices for the minor characters, for example, a yappy, yelping panting dog, a shrieking, squeaking bird and a croaky frog. Emphasise words such as *wailed* and *spat* by raising and lowering your voice as you say the word to mimic those sounds, and raise your voice at the end of questions. Pause for effect before turning a page when the text indicates this with an ellipsis.

Indicate words by moving along them with a finger or pointer as you read, and remember to pause at significant points to ask the children what they think will happen next or to predict a word or phrase, for example: *What do you think will happen to the broom if the frog keeps on jumping on it? What do you think will rise out of the cauldron?*

As you continue to read, ensure that the children understand the text through appropriate comments and queries. For instance: *The dog appeared on thundering paws. What do you think the author means by this? How would you describe the sound of a dog's paws? What do you know about the sound of thunder? Does this knowledge help you to answer the questions?* If necessary, explain language such as *ear-splitting, moors, bog, ditch* and *strode*.

Guided reading

Encourage the children to consider how characters are feeling as the story progresses by asking them how they would feel in a similar situation. For example: *Have you ever enjoyed an exciting ride? Why was it exciting? Have you ever been really frightened by something? What did you do?* Always be prepared to follow the children's comments, interests and ideas when you ask these questions, and encourage respect for differing opinions and aspirations.

Draw attention to the rich and detailed illustrations and discuss how they enhance the story, for instance, explore the image of the *horrible beast* facing the dragon. Ask: *How can you tell that the beast is really the witch's friends? How do you know that they have made use of the cauldron and broom to help make the beast? How can you tell that the witch is helpless? Why is she not using her wand? How can you tell that the dragon is worried?*

Finally, encourage the children to voice their initial impressions of the book.

Subsequent readings

There are many things you may wish to focus on after the initial read-through.

Time passes

Read the story again, this time focusing on how the author and illustrator give clues as to how time passes and landscape and weather change as events unfold. Ask: *What is the weather like when the witch starts her journey? Is it during the day or at night? How does the weather change as the witch flies over the fields? Can we tell what season it is by the crop in the fields? What is the weather like when the witch loses her wand? Do we know what sort of landscape the witch flies over after she finds her wand? Does the story end during the day or at night?* Discuss the role of the illustrations in arriving at answers, supported by words in the text (such as *wind, stormy, moors, mountains* and *cloud*).

A roller-coaster journey!

Ask the children to share experiences of observing, or riding on, roller coasters. Talk about the feelings we experience as we gradually move higher and higher up the track, then fly downwards at great speed only to start climbing again. Read the story together and discuss how the author achieves this effect as she gradually builds her story to an exciting climax. Recall how every time a character climbs aboard the broom we are filled with expectation of what lies ahead, only to have our hopes dashed as, once again, something else is lost. When it seems that this thrilling journey is doomed to end in peril, the courageous efforts of the new-found friends save the day. Ask: *Can you describe the feelings you experience as you read the story? Do your feelings stay the same throughout? Why do you think this story is so exciting?*

Rhyme for a reason

Focus on the importance of rhyme and rhythm in the book. Ask the children to choose a favourite page and read it to them, emphasising the rhythm and rhyming words as you do so. Read the page again, this time together with the class, so that the children can feel the rhythm and rhyme.

Now read the page a third time to the children, substituting rhyming words with non-rhyming words that have similar meanings. Ask: *Which of the two versions that you have heard has rhyming words? Which one do you think sounds best?*

Fact or fantasy?

Establish the meanings of the words 'fact' and 'fantasy'. Talk about how some stories are about everyday events, such as a day at the seaside, whereas others are about imaginary events, often set in magical worlds. Play a simple game with the class to decide which category *Room on the Broom* falls into. Sit the children in a circle with everyday versions of some of the items in the story (for example, a sweeping brush, cooking pan, hat, coat, photograph of a pet cat and wooden spoon), and *Room on the Broom* versions of similar items (such as a broomstick, witch's hat, cloak, model dragon, wand and plastic cauldron, which is obtainable from garden centres), placed at random in the centre. Decide, as a class, which of the objects could be found in a factual setting and which ones belong to a fantasy setting. Use this evidence to help establish why *Room on the Broom* is a fantasy story.

Book review

After discussing the type of story it is, along with the settings, characters, events and effects of pattern and rhyme in detail, invite the children to reconsider their original impressions of the book. Encourage them to voice their opinions with confidence and clarity, referring to the text and illustrations wherever possible. Ask: *Do you still feel the same about this story, or have your opinions changed since our first discussion? Do you think the story works well because it uses rhyme and pattern, or do you think it could be improved in another way? Have your opinions changed about the illustrations now that you have explored them in detail? Was there any part of the story that you did not enjoy? How do you feel about the ending?*

Shared reading

Extract 1

● Display and read an enlarged copy of Extract 1. Invite the children to discuss the information it conveys about the story and characters. Ask: *How soon are we introduced to the main character?* (On line one.) *What do we know about her appearance? From what you have read, and the illustration, do you think she is a wicked or a friendly witch? Who is the other character we meet in this extract?*

● Number each line and highlight the rhyming words to emphasise them. Introduce to the class the notion that the text resembles a poem because of the shape and the regular rhyming words at the end of the lines.

● Together, examine the spelling of the rhyming words and highlight phonemes that have different graphemes, for example: *hat/plait* and *grinned/wind*.

● Focus on the last line and ask: *Does this line make you want to read more? What do you think might happen next?*

Extract 2

● Read an enlarged copy of Extract 2 together and then highlight the rhyming words at the end of the lines. Clap the rhythm as you re-read it, using greater volume to emphasise the rhyming words.

● Discuss the information conveyed by the descriptive words. Ask: *Which words tell us that the beast is really the witch's four friends?* (Underline the words *feathered, furred, four frightful heads* and *wings.*) *Which four words describe the sounds made by the beast?* (They are *yowl, growl, croak* and *shriek.*) Together, decide which friend was responsible for each sound. Locate each of the witch's four friends in the illustration.

● Invite the children to circle words that describe the appearance of the horrible beast and how it moved (such as *rose* and *strode*).

● Focus on the punctuation in the beast's words on the last two lines and discuss the author's reasons for using exclamation marks and capital letters. Encourage the children to pretend to be the beast and, using a suitable voice, say these words with emphasis and volume.

Extract 3

● Display and read an enlarged copy of Extract 3. Encourage the children to use knowledge of high-frequency words and apply existing phonic knowledge to read words such as *stirred* and *cone*, as well as the nonsense sounds of the spell.

● Draw attention to the satisfactory sound created by repeating the word 'found' four times. Elicit that this repetition strengthens the rhythm, making it punchy. Also note that it emphasises a team effort, with them all working together.

● Focus on the nonsense sounds of the spell and emphasise how the repetition of the 'z' sound makes a satisfying jingle. Clap and chant the spell together.

● Discuss how this extract leads us to the ending. Establish whether this is a good ending by discussing the content of the extract. Ask: *Why was the witch casting a spell? How did the four friends help? What happened after the spell was cast?*

● Introduce the notion that the author creates a very satisfying story conclusion that leaves us eager to know what happens on their next broom adventure. Ask: *Do you like this ending? How does it leave you feeling? There is room on the new broom for all, so do you think they might travel together on further adventures? What kinds of problem do you think they'll encounter?*

SECTION
3

Extract 1

The witch had a cat
and a very tall hat,
And long ginger hair
which she wore in a plait.
How the cat purred
and how the witch grinned,
As they sat on their broomstick
and flew through the wind.

But how the witch wailed
and how the cat spat,
When the wind blew so wildly
it blew off the hat.

Text © 2001, Julia Donaldson; Illustration © 2001, Axel Scheffler.

 SCHOLASTIC
www.scholastic.co.uk

READ & RESPOND: Activities based on Room on the Broom

Extract 2

But just as he planned
   to begin on his feast,
From out of a ditch
   rose a horrible beast.
It was tall, dark and sticky,
   and feathered and furred.
It had four frightful heads,
   it had wings like a bird.
And its terrible voice,
   when it started to speak,
Was a yowl and a growl
   and a croak and a shriek.
It dripped and it squelched
   as it strode from the ditch,
And it said to the dragon,
   "Buzz off! –
   THAT'S MY WITCH!"

Text © 2001, Julia Donaldson; Illustration © 2001, Axel Scheffler.

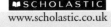

Extract 3

Then she filled up her cauldron
   and said with a grin,
"Find something, everyone,
   throw something in!"
So the frog found a lily,
   the cat found a cone,
The bird found a twig
   and the dog found a bone.

They threw them all in
   and the witch stirred them well,
And while she was stirring
   she muttered a spell.
"Iggety, ziggety, zaggety, ZOOM!"

Then out rose...

...A TRULY
MAGNIFICENT BROOM!

Text © 2001, Julia Donaldson.

PHOTOCOPIABLE

PAGE
10

 SCHOLASTIC
www.scholastic.co.uk
READ & RESPOND: Activities based on Room on the Broom

Plot, character and setting

What happens next?

Objective: To use syntax and context when reading for meaning.
What you need: Copies of *Room on the Broom*, scissors and photocopiable page 15 (one enlarged copy and one per pair).

What to do
● As a class read *Room on the Broom* and discuss how events follow a pattern to create a satisfying story.
● Display an enlarged version of photocopiable page 15. Read the sentence sequence together and discuss whether it tells the story in the correct order.
● Together, decide which two sentences might be appropriate to begin and end the story and number these 1 and 10. Number the remaining sentences from 2 to 9 in the order the story events occur.
● Double-check that the sequence is correct by inviting individuals to stand in a line holding numerals from 1 to 10. Ask each child to read out their corresponding-numbered sentence, starting with sentence 1.
● Cover the class answers. Arrange the children into pairs, providing each with photocopiable page 15 and scissors. Ask them to cut and paste the sentences to order the story events together.
● Bring the class together to share the story sequences. Which are the most accurate? Do they match the class sequence? (The suggested sequence is: 7, 10, 3, 1, 5, 8, 4, 2, 6, 9.)

Differentiation
For older/more confident learners: Ask the children to extend the sentences, adding further details that they remember about the story, without referring to the text.
For younger/less confident learners: Provide the children with a simplified version of the sheet, containing only five sentences for them to sequence.

We can help

Objective: To explain their views to others in a small group, decide how to report the group's views to the class.
What you need: Copies of *Room on the Broom*.
Cross-curricular link: PSHE.

What to do
● Arrange the children into four groups and allocate one of the minor characters (cat, dog, bird and frog) to each group.
● Ask the children to think about their specific character and talk about how they are able to help the witch. Remind them to discuss the whole story so that they include the way that the characters find things for the witch as the story unfolds and then help to create the beast to scare away the dragon towards the end of the story.
● Explain to each group that they need to present their finding about their character's helpfulness to the class, in as clear a way as possible. Invite them to consider the best way to report back. For example, individuals might pretend to be the character at different points in the story and explain how they could help the witch. Alternatively, pairs of children could hold mock TV or radio interviews about how their character saved the witch's life.

Differentiation
For older/more confident learners: Ask the children to invent a short dialogue between two of the characters showing how they feel about a significant story event. (For example, when the frog found the wand would there be profuse thanks from the witch?)
For younger/less confident learners: Support the children by providing prompt questions which they could answer in a simple question and answer session.

Plot, character and setting

Using drama for exploration

> **Objective:** To act out their own and well-known stories, using voices for characters.
> **What you need:** Copies of *Room on the Broom*, photocopiable page 15, props (such as a bench or plank, wooden boxes, cloak, bow, hat and wand) and masks for dog, cat, bird, frog and dragon.
> **Cross-curricular link:** Drama.

What to do
● Encourage the children to work in groups of six to dramatise the story of *Room on the Broom* for the rest of the class.
● Provide copies of the book and the sequence sentences on photocopiable page 15 to help the groups with their planning.
● Ask the groups to begin by making lists of the characters and props needed, talking about how to make props such as a broom to sit on (for example, a long bench or plank with a wooden box at either end).

● Emphasise the need to discuss and try out the voices and movements of the characters and any sound effects (such as yowling, growling, shrieking and wailing).
● Allow time for the children to explore and modify their dramatisations before their performances.
● After each performance, ask the audience to comment on the success of the productions. Have they missed anything? Was anything unclear?

> **Differentiation**
> **For older/more confident learners:** Allow the children to record their performances in order for them to write a review. (How realistic were their characters' voices and movements?)
> **For younger/less confident learners:** Allow the children to dramatise a couple of sections of the story and provide character puppets to help them lose their inhibitions.

Setting detectives

> **Objective:** To visualise and comment on events, characters and ideas, making imaginative links to their own experiences.
> **What you need:** Copies of *Room on the Broom* and photocopiable page 16 (enlarged to A3).

What to do
● Establish with the class what is meant by a 'setting', using the surroundings in which your school is set as an example.
● Explain to the children that they need to imagine they are detectives searching for clues about the setting for *Room on the Broom*.
● Display an enlarged version of photocopiable page 16 and read the headings. Ask what types of things tell us about the 'Landscape'. (For example, is it dry and sandy, or green with mountains and trees?) Establish that 'Growing things' include plants, flowers, trees, bushes and

toadstools, while 'Fairy-tale images' are things we don't see in our own lives (for example, dragons and witches).
● Divide the class into 'detective' groups and hand each group a copy of *Room on the Broom* and the photocopiable sheet. Invite them to examine the 'evidence' in the book and complete the sheet.
● Together, share their findings.

> **Differentiation**
> **For older/more confident learners:** Make the photocopiable sheet more challenging by removing the word bank.
> **For younger/less confident learners:** Simplify the photocopiable sheet for the children by listing appropriate setting words and asking them to tick each as they locate them in the book. Possibly add a few trick words to the list.

Plot, character and setting

The witch and the dragon

Objective: To give some reasons why things happen or characters change.
What you need: Copies of *Room on the Broom* and photocopiable page 17 (one per group).
Cross-curricular link: Drama.

What to do
● With the class, discuss the role of good and bad characters in fairy tales.
● Explore common 'witch' features (such as a hat and cloak) and unusual features (such as a friendly smile and kind words). Establish that this witch is not a typical one.
● Discuss how the dragon changes from fierce to frightened in the story, and encourage the class to decide whether this dragon is typical.
● Put the class into groups and provide photocopiable page 17 for them to discuss and complete. They should circle words to describe the characters of the witch and dragon and write

their own words to describe their appearance and what they might say. Explain that the notes they make will help them to explore the characters.
● Next, invite pairs into the hot-seat and to use their notes to adopt the roles of the witch or dragon, while other group members ask questions about the character's feelings during their eventful encounter.
● Bring the class together to discuss how and why the characters reacted as they did.

Differentiation
For older/more confident learners: Invite the children to conduct question and answer sessions to establish why things happened (for example, 'Why did your hat blow off?', 'Because the wind…').
For younger/less confident learners: Allow the children to draw pictures of the witch and dragon and concentrate on completing the first two sections of the photocopiable sheet.

A home for the witch

Objective: To engage with books through exploring and enacting interpretations.
What you need: Copies of *Room on the Broom*, recycled material (such as coloured scraps of fabrics), story-linked small-world resources (such as a doll, cat, dog, bird, frog and dragon toys) and a washing-up brush.
Cross-curricular link: Art and design.

What to do
● Read *Room on the Broom* together and talk about where the witch might live. Look closely at the illustrations and recall past fairy tales containing witches, such as 'Hansel and Gretel', 'Snow White' and 'Rapunzel'.
● Explore the book illustrations for inspiration, for example, maybe the witch lives in a cave in the snow-covered mountains or a house in the deep dark forest. Ask: *What will the house look*

like? Could the witch live in the castle? Does the witch live alone?
● Invite the children to work in groups to create a suitable home for the witch, using the materials supplied to build her home (such as using fabric draped over chairs to form caves).
● Dress a doll as a witch using black fabric, and convert a washing-up brush into a broom. Then introduce the doll and other small-world resources, so the children can re-enact the story starting from the witch's home.

Differentiation
For older/more confident learners: Invite the children to build the story set, including homes for the other characters so they can re-enact the story.
For younger/less confident learners: Provide the children with a list of potential homes from the book asking them to choose one, then allow them to draw the exterior and one room in the witch's house.

Plot, character and setting

New endings

> **Objective:** To ensure that everyone contributes, allocate tasks, and consider alternatives and reach agreement.
> **What you need:** Copies of *Room on the Broom* and photocopiable page 18 (one copy for each group, cut into cards).
> **Cross-curricular link:** Drama.

What to do

● Discuss the story ending and decide whether it is a good one. Encourage the children to give reasons for their answers.

● Talk about how the children might feel if the ending had been different. Perhaps they feel that the original ending is best? Explain that they are going to explore different endings to see if their feelings change.

● Divide the class into groups and invite them to choose one of the alternative event cards created from photocopiable page 18. Explain that the cards contain new ideas for an event that might change the story ending and they need to think how the story might end differently.

● Ask the groups to discuss possible endings based on their chosen scenario, encouraging them to make active individual contributions. Invite them to dramatise these ideas and reach a joint conclusion.

● Once they have composed their ending, bring the class together and allow each group to perform their ideas.

● Decide on a favourite ending by a vote of hands. Include the original ending in this vote.

> **Differentiation**
> **For older/more confident learners:** Ask the children to invent their own alternative story endings without using one of the alternative event cards supplied.
> **For younger/less confident learners:** Provide the children with a list of possible small story-step routes and allow them to select and piece them together, filling in details where possible.

New brooms

> **Objective:** To tell real and imagined stories using the conventions of familiar story language.
> **What you need:** Copies of *Room on the Broom*, drawing tools and materials.

What to do

● Revisit the children's work on the story setting (see the 'Setting detectives' activity) and ask them to consider what would happen if the story were set in another fantasy world (for example, deep under the sea or out in space).

● Discuss difficulties that might arise in a new setting. For instance, how would the broom fly under the sea or out in space?

● Divide the class into pairs and ask them to design a broom that could be used in a different setting, for example, a submarine broom or a rocket broom. Provide lots of drawing tools and materials so that the children can create diagrams.

● Once the broom designs are complete, suggest that each pair invent a short story involving the witch and this new broom.

● Ask for volunteers to show their broom diagrams and read their stories to the class. Encourage them to use story language, particularly to define the beginning and end of the story.

> **Differentiation**
> **For older/more confident learners:** Invite the children to consider other aspects of the story that might change if it took place in another setting (for example, encounters with aliens or deep-sea creatures).
> **For younger/less confident learners:** Provide the children with a list of features and gadgets they could add to their brooms and allow them to work in larger groups, with each child taking a small section of the story to develop.

What happens next?

● Cut out the ten sentences and arrange them in the correct order to tell the story.

A bird flew down from a tree with the bow in her beak and there was room on the broom for her.
A dragon wanted to eat the witch with chips for his tea.
The witch was flying on her broom when her bow blew away.
The broom was so full that it snapped and they all fell down into a bog.
The witch was flying on her broom when she let go of her wand.
The four friends pretended to be a horrible beast and the dragon flew away.
The witch was flying on her broom when her hat blew off.
A frog jumped out of a pond with the wand in his hand and there was room on the broom for him.
The witch cast a spell to make a new broom and they all flew away together.
A dog came out of the bushes with the hat in his mouth and there was room on the broom for him.

Setting detectives

● Examine the book for 'evidence' of the story setting and place your clues under the appropriate headings.

● The word bank is there to help you, but also try to identify your own clues.

Landscape	Weather	Growing things	Animals, insects and birds	Fairy-tale images
cornfields	clouds	poppies	cat	dragon

Word bank

mountains   heron   moon   trees   dog   owl
toadstools   sheep   squirrel   cauldron   haystacks
broom   wind   crow   forest   green bird   castle   witch
wand   rain   pond   river   frog   ditch   cone   bog
ant   beast   star   dragonfly   snow   lilies

The witch and the dragon

● Complete the table below, making notes about the witch and the dragon. Use these notes when you take the hot-seat.

Question	Witch	Dragon
Circle the words that describe the character.	wicked friendly cruel kind scary funny	fierce friendly scary kind cowardly brave
Write words to describe the character's appearance.		
Write some words the character might use/ say.		

Illustrations © 2001, Axel Scheffler.

Plot, character and setting

New endings

● Cut out the boxes. Select one of these alternative event cards and consider how this would have changed the ending of the story.

The witch forgot the spell and it all went wrong!
Out of the cauldron came…

Oh dear! The new broom only had two seats. There was no room for the cat, so…

Out of the cauldron came a truly magnificent broom, with legs and arms and a very loud voice!

Suddenly the dragon appeared in the sky.
"Is there room on the broom for me?" he whimpered.

"Don't go this way" hooted an owl.
"A huge giant lives in those mountains."
But it was too late…

"I have one more spell to cast", chuckled the witch.
"Wiggle, woggle, waggle, woo!" Then…

Flash! Crash! A storm began.
Plip, plop came the big raindrops.

SCHOLASTIC
www.scholastic.co.uk

Talk about it

This is me!

Objective: To explore the effects of patterns of language and repeated words and phrases.
What you need: Copies of *Room on the Broom* and photocopiable page 22 (one enlarged copy and one per group).

What to do
● Read *Room on the Broom* together before drawing attention to the regular pattern of the words the animals use to describe themselves (for example, *"I am a dog, as keen as can be"* and *"I am a frog, as clean as can be"*). Discuss how effective it is to have rhyming words in the middle of a sentence.
● List the rhyming words from the animals in this sequence (*keen, green, clean, mean*) and chant them as a string.
● Display an enlarged copy of photocopiable page 22 and read the top line of each couplet together. Focus on the underlined words and talk about possible rhyming words. Write a class list on the board.
● Divide the class into groups and hand each a copy of the sheet to complete.
● Ask the groups to read their completed couplets to the class in an interesting way, for example, with the children using appropriate voices for the characters. Encourage emphasis of the rhyming word in each sentence.

Differentiation
For older/more confident learners: Encourage the children to create two of their own couplets with internal rhyming descriptive words and share them with the class.
For younger/less confident learners: Allow the children to focus on completing two of the couplets and to draw pictures to accompany them.

One good turn deserves another

Objective: To tell stories and describe incidents from their own experience in an audible voice.
What you need: Copies of *Room on the Broom*, access to books, computers and other information about people who help us.
Cross-curricular link: PSHE.

What to do
● Read *Room on the Broom* and, with the class, identify the roles of the animals who rode on the witch's broom. Discuss how each animal helped the witch by finding her possessions and creating a beast to frighten the dragon.
● Ask the children about ways in which they help their friends and how their friends help them. Encourage individuals to share their experiences with the class.
● Talk about how the witch responded to the kindness of the animals by letting them ride on her broom, and eventually creating a new broom for everyone. Discuss ways in which we can return a kindness.
● Extend the discussion further by considering specific helpful people, such as the different emergency services (fire, police and ambulance services).
● Divide the class into groups and ask them to research one of these emergency services, using appropriate websites and books.
● Encourage each group to present their findings to the class and provide constructive feedback.

Differentiation
For older/more confident learners: Invite the children to take on the role of a member of one of the emergency services and to answer questions in the hot-seat.
For younger/less confident learners: To help structure their research, provide the children with prompt questions, such as: What equipment do they use?

Talk about it

The broom that had room

> **Objective:** To make predictions showing an understanding of ideas, events and characters.
> **What you need:** Copies of *Room on the Broom* and photocopiable page 23 (one enlarged copy and one per child).

What to do
● Identify the rhyming words in the title. Read the story to the class, pausing before an obvious rhyming word so that the children can make a prediction, for example, *the cat found a cone… and the dog found a…?*
● Display an enlarged version of photocopiable page 23, covering the right column. Read the words on the left, pointing out these are from the story. Explain that each word needs matching to a rhyming word, which you are hiding.
● Ask the children to predict the rhyming words, also taken from the story. Write the most popular choices in the empty centre column.

● Display the whole page, checking whether the predicted words written in the centre column appear on the right. Reinforce the rhymes from the story.
● Read one of the rhyming pairs and substitute one rhyming word with a non-rhyming word, for example, 'cat/hat', 'cat/wind' to emphasise the satisfying effect of rhyme.
● Discuss how sounds can be the same in some words but spellings may be different, for example, *furred/bird*. Identify rhyming words with matching (then differing) letter combinations.

> **Differentiation**
> **For older/more confident learners:** Ask the children to use the rhyming words on the sheet to create new rhyming sentences.
> **For younger/less confident learners:** Allow the children to focus on identifying three of the rhyming pairs.

Whoosh! they were gone!

> **Objective:** To present part of traditional stories, their own stories or work drawn from different parts of the curriculum for members of their own class.
> **What you need:** Copies of *Room on the Broom*, percussion/musical instruments and everyday items (such as bottles of water and fabric).
> **Cross-curricular links:** Drama, music.

What to do
● Read the three sections of the story that start with *"Down!" cried the witch* and end *whoosh! they were gone.* Talk about the contextual clues as to sounds that might be heard, such as the dog's *thundering paws*, the witch tapping her broomstick and the bird shrieking and flapping.
● Discuss how to create these sounds, for example, using children's voices to *shriek* and *whoosh*, shaking fabric for the flapping wings, beating drums for thunder.

● Divide the class into three groups with each one focusing on dramatising one of the three sections (involving the dog, bird or frog) with accompanying sounds. Provide each group with a copy of the book and suggest that they choose a narrator.
● After giving them time to prepare, gather the class in a large circle, read the story and ask the three groups to move to the centre to perform their re-enactments at the correct time.

> **Differentiation**
> **For older/more confident learners:** Invite the children to add sound effects to dramatisations of two other sections of *Room on the Broom*.
> **For younger/less confident learners:** Help the children to create suitable sounds by highlighting all the key words in the text that indicate sounds are required (such as *cried*, *shriek*, *flapped* and *tapped*).

Talk about it

The witch and the troll

> **Objective:** To spell with increasing accuracy and confidence, drawing on word recognition and knowledge of word structure, and spelling patterns.
> **What you need:** Copies of *Room on the Broom* and photocopiable page 24 (one enlarged copy and one per child).

What to do
● Read *Room on the Broom* and recall previous discussions about rhyme. Find examples in the book (and possibly photocopiable page 23) of rhyming words ending with the same sounds (phonemes) but with different ways of spelling these sounds (graphemes), for example, 'h**igher**' 'f**ire**'.
● Write on the board 'This is a story about a witch who had a broom which was red.' Highlight the words 'witch' and 'which' and ask the children what they notice about them. Encourage them to discover for themselves that they sound like the same word but have a different spelling and meaning.
● Display an enlarged version of photocopiable page 24 and read the first three sentences. Highlight the word that fits the context and talk about the meaning of the other word.
● Arrange the children into pairs, then provide them with the photocopiable sheet to discuss and complete.

> **Differentiation**
> **For older/more confident learners:** Invite the children to create sentences containing the nine words that they did not circle on the sheet.
> **For younger/less confident learners:** Let the children concentrate on completing about half of the sheet.

That's another story

> **Objective:** To tell real and imagined stories using the conventions of familiar story language.
> **What you need:** Copies of *Room on the Broom*.

What to do
● Read *Room on the Broom* and ask the class to identify the five characters other than the witch (cat, dog, bird, frog and dragon).
● Talk about the part each of these characters plays in shaping the story's direction.
● Invite someone to choose a character from the list, for instance the frog. As a class, make up a version of the story from the frog's viewpoint, starting with conventional language such as, 'Once upon a time a frog found a wand in a pond'.
● Discuss how the frog might feel when he discovers the wand. Ask: *Would he know what it was? Would he want to make spells with it? Would he try to find the owner?*
● Divide the class into five groups. Invite each group to focus on a different listed character and to make up their own version of the story from this character's point of view. Promote use of conventional story language.
● When their stories are complete, invite each group to tell or re-enact their versions to the rest of the class.
● Encourage the other children to comment constructively on the stories.

> **Differentiation**
> **For older/more confident learners:** Ask the children to write at least two stories (each for a different animal) and to transform them into an illustrated book of stories (perhaps entitled 'The cat's tale', 'The frog's tale').
> **For younger/less confident learners:** Suggest that the children draw a picture of their chosen character and help them to write a simple story, roughly about one paragraph.

SECTION
5

This is me!

● Read the couplets below. Circle the word in brackets which rhymes with the underlined word in the line above.

"I am a dog, as **keen** as can be."

"I am a giant, as (tall / mean / kind) as can be."

"I am a troll, as **bad** as can be."

"I am a cat, as (happy / glad / cheery) as can be."

"I am a snowman, as **white** as can be."

"I am a star, as (twinkly / silver / bright) as can be."

"I am a crocodile, as **snappy** as can be."

"I am a dog, as (hairy / yappy / scruffy) as can be."

Illustration © 2012, Mike Lacey (Beehive Illustration).

The broom that had room

● Write some words in the centre column that rhyme with the words listed on the left. Check your answers.

broom		room
cat		hat
wand		pond
shriek		beak
grinned		wind
feast		beast
bird		furred

Talk about it

The witch and the troll

● Both words in the brackets sound the same. Read each sentence and circle the words with the correct spelling and meaning.

Once upon a time there was a happy (which / witch).

She had a shiny new (red / read) broom.

An ugly troll (through / threw) a big stone at the witch.

The witch dropped the broom on the (flaw / floor).

The broom turned into (too / two) brooms.

One broom began to beat the troll's ugly (tows / toes).

One broom squashed the troll's big long (knows / nose).

The troll gave a loud (wail / whale) and jumped into his pool.

The witch (made / maid) a spell to mend the broom.

Illustration © 2012, Mike Lacey (Beehive Illustration).

Get writing

Witch and chips

Objective: To use capital letters and full stops when punctuating simple sentences.
What you need: Copies of *Room on the Broom*.

What to do
● Read *Room on the Broom* with the class and then focus on the words of the dragon. Remind the children of the importance of starting sentences with a capital letter and ending with a full stop. Ask them to find examples of this punctuation on the page (spread 8).
● Draw attention to the words *WITCH AND CHIPS* and discuss the fact that they are in the middle of a sentence. Explain that capital letters like this emphasise certain words. Try saying the sentence together with the class, raising voices for the words in capitals. Discuss how this serves to make the dragon sound very fierce.

● Now read the words of the beast on the last two lines of the next page (spread 9) and discuss the use of capitals and exclamations. (Is the beast shouting?)
● Ask the children to write their own versions of the dragon's words. Remind them to write in sentences with a capital letter at the beginning and a full stop at the end.

Differentiation
For older/more confident learners: Encourage the children to use further punctuation in their sentences, such as speech marks and exclamation marks.
For younger/less confident learners: Display simple sentences to describe the encounter of the witch and dragon, without punctuation. Ask the children to write them out, adding a capital letter at the beginning and a full stop at the end.

Which words?

Objective: To find and use new and interesting words and phrases, including story language.
What you need: Copies of *Room on the Broom* and photocopiable page 28 (one enlarged copy and one per child).

What to do
● Read *Room on the Broom* and draw the children's attention to the rhyme.
● Discuss how the author's choice of words help us to imagine the characters and objects, the way they look, sound and feel.
● Search for effective words used by the author to describe sounds (for example, *purred* and *wailed*) and movement (such as *bounded* and *clambered*).
● Display an enlarged version of photocopiable page 28 and ask individuals to add naming words to the top box. Continue by adding describing

words in the appropriate columns. Discuss the importance of making writing interesting by choosing and using suitable words.
● Provide individuals with the photocopiable sheet to complete. Explain that the poem they write can be about any character or object from the story. Emphasise that the words they have collected can be used in their poem, but that they should try to incorporate interesting words of their own as well.
● Bring the class together to share their poems.

Differentiation
For older/more confident learners: Invite the children to write a descriptive poem about their own imaginary characters (such as a wizard or rabbit).
For younger/less confident learners: Ask the children to focus on drawing a picture of one of the characters and to write a simple sentence to describe their appearance.

Get writing

Book review

> **Objective:** To independently choose what to write about, plan and follow it through.
> **What you need:** Copies of *Room on the Broom* and photocopiable page 29 (one enlarged copy and one per child).

What to do

● Read *Room on the Broom* and discuss the children's overall impressions.

● Recall previous examples of books the author and illustrator have worked on together, such as *The Gruffalo* and *A Squash and a Squeeze*. Talk about the role of the author's rhyme and the illustrator's quirky characters and attention to detail, in supporting the children's enjoyment of the books. Make comparisons with *Room on the Broom*.

● Explain the purpose of a book review and read sample reviews from the back covers of the children's favourite books. Suggest that the children write reviews for *Room on the Broom*.

● Together, read through an enlarged version of photocopiable page 29, a section at a time. Talk about the merits or possible shortcomings of the rhyming text, illustrations and characters. Discuss what is meant by a star rating.

● Provide individuals with photocopiable page 29, asking them to plan and write an independent book review.

> **Differentiation**
> **For older/more confident learners:** Invite the children to review a story by a different author and illustrator, modifying the sheet accordingly.
> **For younger/less confident learners:** Allow the children to focus on reviewing a favourite event in the book (for example, when the 'beast' scares away the dragon). Ask them to draw a picture and write about it.

My special spell

> **Objective:** To make adventurous word and language choices appropriate to the style and purpose of the text.
> **What you need:** Copies of *Room on the Broom* and photocopiable page 30 (one enlarged copy and one per child).

What to do

● Talk about how spells are used in stories and the type of characters who might use them, such as witches and wizards.

● Read the last section of the book that describes how the witch makes her spell and make a list of the ingredients on the board. Discuss the reason for the spell (for a magnificent new broom).

● Read the chant for the witch's spell with the class and recall other magic spell chants (such as 'Abracadabra' and 'Hocus Pocus'). Draw attention to the satisfying repetition of nonsense sounds (the repetition of the 'z' sound).

● Display an enlarged version of photocopiable page 30 and work through it together, inventing a magic spell for the class (for example, to whisk them to a fantasy land).

● Provide individuals with the photocopiable sheet to complete, emphasising the importance of using magical words and nonsense sounds.

● Bring the class together to share their spells. Collectively decide which spells are the most exciting and use the most imaginative language.

> **Differentiation**
> **For older/more confident learners:** Encourage the children to compile their ideas into an illustrated book of magic spells.
> **For younger/less confident learners:** Let the children concentrate on writing simple chants, encouraging them to spell words according to their levels of phonic awareness.

Get writing

Witch characters

Objective: To draw on knowledge and experience of texts in deciding and planning what and how to write.
What you need: Copies of *Room on the Broom*, a selection of storybooks containing witches, dressing-up clothes and props associated with witches (such as potion bottles, black cloaks, hats, cauldrons, toy cats and frogs).
Cross-curricular link: Drama.

What to do

● Read *Room on the Broom* and invite the children to explore the illustrations for clues that the main character is a witch (for example, a wand, a black hat and cloak).
● Explore witches in other stories by looking through a selection of fiction books and making a class list of items associated with them.
● Using the fiction books, make another class list of words associated with the appearance, behaviour and personality of witches (such as

good, bad, wicked, ugly, crazy, silly, smart, funny and amazing).
● Divide the children into groups and suggest they dress one group member as a witch using the props supplied.
● Next, ask each group to write a descriptive paragraph about their witch character in the first person, beginning, 'My name is… and I am…' Encourage them to refer to the class lists to help them.
● Encourage the children to take turns to read their descriptions to the class. Discuss which is the most popular and why.

Differentiation
For older/more confident learners: Ask the children to write a witch story, using their character descriptions.
For younger/less confident learners: Allow the children to write simple sentences to just describe the witch in *Room on the Broom*.

A truly magnificent broom

Objective: To select from different presentational features to suit particular purposes on paper and on screen.
What you need: Copies of *Room on the Broom*, writing and drawing materials, access to computers and examples of magazine advertisements.
Cross-curricular links: Art and design, ICT.

What to do

● Encourage the class to explore the *truly magnificent broom* illustration at the end of the story. Discuss special features included for the broom passengers, such as the frog's shower and bird's nest.
● Talk about features the children would include on a magnificent broom.
● Next, explore magazine adverts showing a range of products for sale and talk about the information they contain (such as the product name and price). Ask questions to encourage the

children to consider how adverts are designed to attract readers (for example, using photographs, punchy catchphrases, different fonts, and so on).
● Divide the class into groups and ask each group to design an advert for a magnificent broom. Remind them to consider who will be buying their broom and how they can encourage these buyers to choose their model of broom. Explain that they can create their design on paper or computer.
● Display the designs and discuss their merits and shortcomings.

Differentiation
For older/more confident learners: Invite the children to write a set of instructions showing how to build the broom featured in their advert.
For younger/less confident learners: Ask the children to draw their own broom and write one sentence about it.

Get writing

Which words?

● Gather descriptive words from *Room on the Broom* and use them, along with your own words, to write a poem.

List the names of the characters and objects from the story.
frog   broomstick

Write words that are used to describe the characters and objects in the story.

'Sound' words	'Sight' words	'Touch' words	'Movement' words
purred	frightful	sticky	fluttered

Add some of your own descriptive words.

● Now use this information to write a poem about one of the characters or objects on the back of the sheet.

READ & RESPOND: Activities based on *Room on the Broom*

Get writing

Book review

● Plan and write a book review for *Room on the Broom.* Finish the sentences below giving your opinions.

Author and illustrator

I think the way the author has written this book is _____

_____

I think the illustrations are _____

_____

Characters

My favourite character is _____

because _____

My least favourite character is _____

because _____

Rhyme

I think that the rhymes make this book _____

My favourite rhyming words in the book are _____

_____

My rating

Rate the story out of five by shading the stars accordingly.

☆ ☆ ☆ ☆ ☆

My special spell

● Create your own witch's spell by completing the sections below.

What is the name of your special spell?

_____

Draw the ingredients in the cauldron.

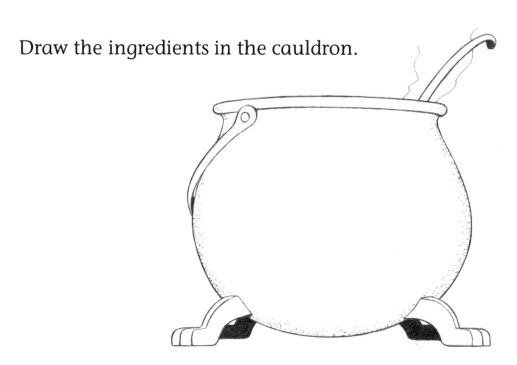

List the ingredients for your special spell, including amounts.

_____

_____

Write the chant to make your special spell work.

_____

_____

What is the purpose of your special spell? What will it create or do?

_____

_____

Illustration © 2012, Mike Lacey (Beehive Illustration).

Assessment

Assessment advice

Ongoing formative assessments of individual achievements and progress in literacy are an essential component of the planning and assessment cycle. They enable teachers to make detailed judgements regarding a child's progress towards specific learning targets, and provide supportive evidence when ensuring that future learning activities are planned at an appropriate level. Assessment outcomes are invaluable in determining new individual targets. Reports and assessments should be based on clear evidence arising from observations and examples of actual work completed.

Formative assessments build up gradually and should be created from a variety of sources, such as observations, contributions to classroom discussions, peer group interaction and analysis of children's practical work. The importance of peer- and self-assessment should not be underestimated. The activities in this book are designed to be assessed using a combination of these methods.

Each activity in the book has a clear assessable learning objective which represents what a child should know, or be able to do, by the end of that activity. Informing children of these objectives before an activity begins is essential in order to help them to recognise their involvement and take ownership of their own learning. At the end of each activity there should be time for reflection, when children can revisit the learning objective and discuss whether or not they think they have achieved it. This helps them to recognise the relevance of assessment in planning the next steps in learning.

You can use the assessment activity on photocopiable page 32 as part of a record of individual progress. It is also a useful tool for assessing a child's ability to plan and write a story on a given theme.

Zoom on the broom

> **Assessment focus:** To sustain form in narrative, including use of person and time.
> **What you need:** Copies of *Room on the Broom* and photocopiable page 32 (one enlarged copy and one per child).

What to do
● Read *Room on the Broom* with the class and discuss the consequences of the witch's chaotic journey on her broomstick as she loses items along the way. Talk about the outcomes of events and the ultimate resolution.
● Invite the children to write a story about another adventure aboard a new broom, involving an unusual setting, a quirky main character and some interesting minor characters. Allow time for the children to discuss their initial ideas with one another.
● Display an enlarged version of photocopiable page 32 and read through it together. Using one of the children's suggestions as an example, fill in the boxes together, modifying and extending ideas.
● Provide each child with a copy of the sheet to plan their own story. As the children are planning, interact with individuals to support their ideas. Encourage them to focus on structure and form within the story by including appropriate opening and closing words and the use of connective words (such as 'then' and 'next', to note the smooth passage of time between events).

Zoom on the broom

● Plan and write your own adventure story about an exciting journey on a broom.

Title:

Setting:

Main character:

Other characters:

Beginning (Make a note of words to use to begin your story. How will you introduce the characters?)

Middle (Make a note of two exciting events that will happen on the journey.)

1.

2.

End (Make a note of words to use at the end. What will be the outcome? Will it be happy or sad?)